First published in Great Britain in 1997 by Brockhampton Press, 20 Bloomsbury
Street, London WC1B 3QA, a member of the Hodder Headline Group.

Compilation and selection copyright © 1997 Brockhampton Press

Photographs copyright © Marc Henrie 1997

ISBN 1 86019 761 2

A copy of the CIP data is available from the British Library upon request.

Produced for Brockhampton Press by Flame Tree Publishing,
a part of the Foundry Creative Media Company Limited,
The Long House, Antrobus Road, Chiswick, London W4 5HY.

Printed and bound in UAE by Oriental Press.

THE ULTIMATE
CAT
& KITTEN
ADDRESS
BOOK

Brockhampton Press

NAME & ADDRESS

Mrs C Ayling
1 Rawnook Rd
Salendine Nook
Huddersfield
N. Yorks

TELEPHONE

01484 656 665

NAME & ADDRESS

TELEPHONE

NAME & ADDRESS

TELEPHONE

NAME & ADDRESS

TELEPHONE

NAME & ADDRESS

TELEPHONE

NAME & ADDRESS

TELEPHONE

ALWAYS GRACEFUL AND elegant, the cat is a study of beauty in motion. The powerful muscles of its long, lithe body undulate under the soft fur, which is often exquisitely marked. When it sleeps, its body curves into a graceful arc. Perhaps the most striking things about a cat are its suppleness and grace of movement and the amazing flexibility of its body.

It is easy to see why the rabble dislike cats.
A cat is beautiful; it suggests
ideas of luxury, cleanliness,
voluptuous pleasures . . . .
Charles Baudelaire

NAME & ADDRESS TELEPHONE

NAME & ADDRESS TELEPHONE

NAME & ADDRESS TELEPHONE

NAME & ADDRESS TELEPHONE

NAME & ADDRESS TELEPHONE

NAME & ADDRESS TELEPHONE

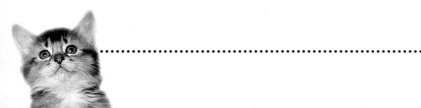

THE CAT, aristocrat both in type and origin, which has been so greatly maligned, deserves our respect at least.
Alexandre Dumas

A house without a cat, a well-fed, well-petted, and properly revered cat, may be a perfect house, perhaps, but how can it prove its title?
Mark Twain

NAME & ADDRESS   TELEPHONE

NAME & ADDRESS   TELEPHONE

NAME & ADDRESS   TELEPHONE

NAME & ADDRESS   TELEPHONE

NAME & ADDRESS   TELEPHONE

NAME & ADDRESS   TELEPHONE

A

NAME & ADDRESS   TELEPHONE

NAME & ADDRESS   TELEPHONE

NAME & ADDRESS   TELEPHONE

NAME & ADDRESS   TELEPHONE

NAME & ADDRESS   TELEPHONE

NAME & ADDRESS   TELEPHONE

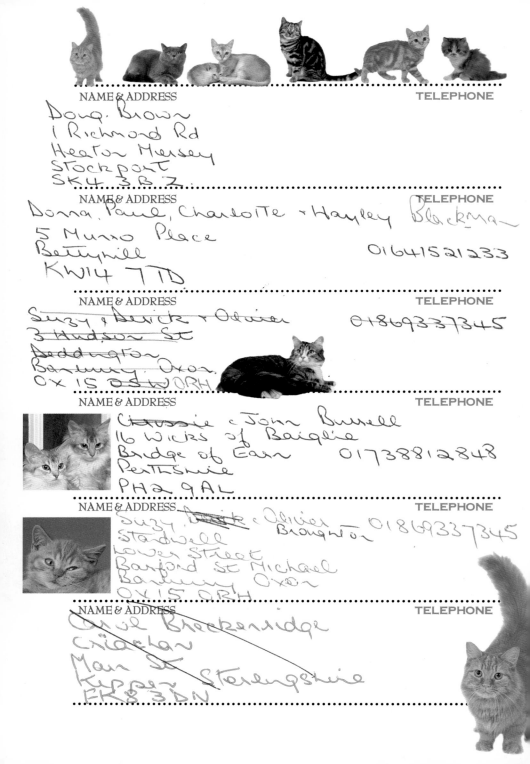

NAME & ADDRESS — **TELEPHONE**

Doug. Brown
1 Richmond Rd
Heaton Mersey
Stockport
SK4 3BZ

NAME & ADDRESS — **TELEPHONE**

Donna, Paul, Charlotte + Hayley Blackman
5 Munro Place
Bettyhill
KW14 7TD
01641521233

NAME & ADDRESS — **TELEPHONE**

Suzy + Derrick + Olivier   01869337345
3 Hudson St
Deddington
Banbury. Oxon.
OX15 0SW 0RH

NAME & ADDRESS — **TELEPHONE**

Carrie John Burrell
16 Wicks of Baiglie
Bridge of Earn   01738812848
Perthshire
PH2 9AL

NAME & ADDRESS — **TELEPHONE**

Suzy Derrick + Olivier — 01869337345
Stadwell   Broughton
Lower Street
Barford St Michael
Banbury Oxon
OX15 0RH

NAME & ADDRESS — **TELEPHONE**

Anil Breckenridge
Crieclan
Main St
Kippen Stirlingshire
FK8 3DN

ACCORDING TO TRADITION, the Manx Cat was the last animal to enter Noah's Ark. The pair insisted on having one last mousing trip before they went aboard. As the rains began to fall more heavily, they rushed on to the Ark, but their tails were caught and cut off as Noah shut the doors behind them. This is why Manx Cats to this day have no tail.

We brought with us in the ship a cat, a most amiable cat and greatly loved by us; but he grew to great bulk through the eating of fish.
St Brendan

NAME & ADDRESS   TELEPHONE

NAME & ADDRESS   TELEPHONE

NAME & ADDRESS   TELEPHONE

NAME & ADDRESS   TELEPHONE

NAME & ADDRESS   TELEPHONE

NAME & ADDRESS   TELEPHONE

NAME & ADDRESS   TELEPHONE

NAME & ADDRESS   TELEPHONE

NAME & ADDRESS   TELEPHONE

NAME & ADDRESS   TELEPHONE

NAME & ADDRESS   TELEPHONE

NAME & ADDRESS   TELEPHONE

NAME & ADDRESS   TELEPHONE

· ·

NAME & ADDRESS   TELEPHONE

· ·

NAME & ADDRESS   TELEPHONE

· ·

NAME & ADDRESS   TELEPHONE

· ·

NAME & ADDRESS   TELEPHONE

· ·

B

I HAD TACKED IT TOGETHER (and the beauty of this fine lace is that, when it is wet, it goes into a very little space), and put it to soak in milk . . . . On my return I found pussy on the table, looking very like a thief, but gulping very uncomfortably . . . all at once I looked and saw the cup of milk empty – cleaned out!
Elizabeth Gaskell

The cat shuts its eyes while it steals the cream.
Proverb

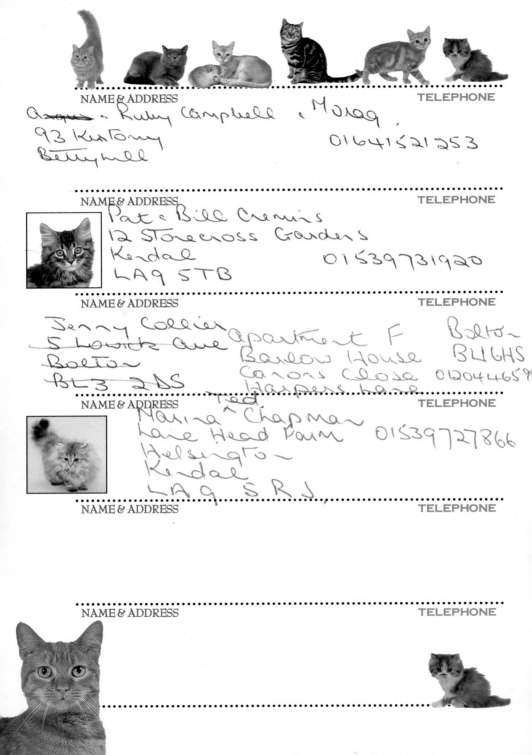

NAME & ADDRESS   **TELEPHONE**

Agnes ~ Ruby Campbell , Morag ,
93 Kirktomy
Bettyhill
01641 521 253

NAME & ADDRESS   **TELEPHONE**

Pat & Bill Cremins
12 Stonecross Gardens
Kendal
LA9 5TB
01539 731920

NAME & ADDRESS   **TELEPHONE**

Jenny Collier
5 Howick Ave
Bolton
BL3 2DS

apartment F   Bolton
Barlow House   BL4 6HS
Canons Close   01204 4658
Harpers Lane

NAME & ADDRESS   **TELEPHONE**

Marina & Ted Chapman
Lane Head Farm   01539 727866
Helsington
Kendal
LA9 5RJ

NAME & ADDRESS   **TELEPHONE**

NAME & ADDRESS   **TELEPHONE**

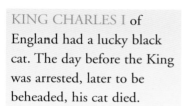

KING CHARLES I of England had a lucky black cat. The day before the King was arrested, later to be beheaded, his cat died.

If the guests at a dinner party number an 'unlucky 13', the Savoy Hotel in London uses a black cat carved from wood – christened Kaspar – to make up the numbers. He sits at the table with the guests and is served food along with everyone else.

NAME & ADDRESS   TELEPHONE

....

NAME & ADDRESS   TELEPHONE

....

NAME & ADDRESS   TELEPHONE

....

NAME & ADDRESS   TELEPHONE

....

NAME & ADDRESS   TELEPHONE

....

NAME & ADDRESS   TELEPHONE

....

NAME & ADDRESS   TELEPHONE

NAME & ADDRESS   TELEPHONE

NAME & ADDRESS   TELEPHONE

NAME & ADDRESS   TELEPHONE

NAME & ADDRESS   TELEPHONE

NAME & ADDRESS   TELEPHONE

NAME & ADDRESS   TELEPHONE

NAME & ADDRESS   TELEPHONE

NAME & ADDRESS   TELEPHONE

NAME & ADDRESS   TELEPHONE

NAME & ADDRESS   TELEPHONE

NAME & ADDRESS   TELEPHONE

*RESCUED A LITTLE KITTEN that
was perched on the sill of the round
window at the sink over the gas jet, and
dared not jump down . . . I make a
note of it because of her gratitude.*
Gerard Manley Hopkins

*Cats are a mysterious kind of folk.
There is more passing in their minds
than we are aware of.*
Sir Walter Scott

NAME & ADDRESS / **TELEPHONE**

Anne & Gilbert Dickinson
5 Jennings Terrace
Kendal
LA9 4ET

NAME & ADDRESS / **TELEPHONE**

Ken & ~~Rose~~ Dawson
Old School House
Kentmere
Kendal   LA8 9JN

01539821157

NAME & ADDRESS / **TELEPHONE**

Margaret Dugdale
9 Curson Rise
Kendal
LA9 7PN

01539723737

NAME & ADDRESS / **TELEPHONE**

Marjorie & Jack Dixon
Ivy Cottage
Scarbskerry

NAME & ADDRESS / **TELEPHONE**

NAME & ADDRESS / **TELEPHONE**

THE ANCIENT EGYPTIANS

revered the cat goddess Bastet (or Bast), also known as Sekhmet. As Bastet she was protective, but as Sekhmet she was bloodthirsty and believed to be responsible for the plague. These two incarnations represented the two faces of the sun: Bastet embodied the warming, life-giving properties of the sun; Sekhmet the destructive, searing heat. Followers of Bastet made her offerings of mummified cats and bronze effigies of herself. Her cult lasted for over 1000 years.

NAME & ADDRESS   TELEPHONE

· ·
NAME & ADDRESS   TELEPHONE

· ·
NAME & ADDRESS   TELEPHONE

· ·
NAME & ADDRESS   TELEPHONE

· ·
NAME & ADDRESS   TELEPHONE

· ·
NAME & ADDRESS   TELEPHONE

· ·

D

LIKE THOSE GREAT SPHINXES *lounging through eternity in noble attitudes upon the desert sand, they gaze in curiosity at nothing, calm and wise.*
Charles Baudelaire

Thou art the Great Cat, the avenger of the Dos, and the judge of words, and the president of the sovereign chiefs and the governor of the Holy Circle; thou art indeed the Great Cat.
Inscription on the royal tomb at Thebes, Ancient Egypt

NAME & ADDRESS   TELEPHONE

NAME & ADDRESS   TELEPHONE

ᴺᴱ & ADDRESS   TELEPHONE

NAME & ADDRESS   TELEPHONE

NAME & ADDRESS   TELEPHONE

NAME & ADDRESS   TELEPHONE

NAME & ADDRESS   TELEPHONE

NAME & ADDRESS   TELEPHONE

NAME & ADDRESS   TELEPHONE

NAME & ADDRESS   TELEPHONE

NAME & ADDRESS   TELEPHONE

NAME & ADDRESS   TELEPHONE

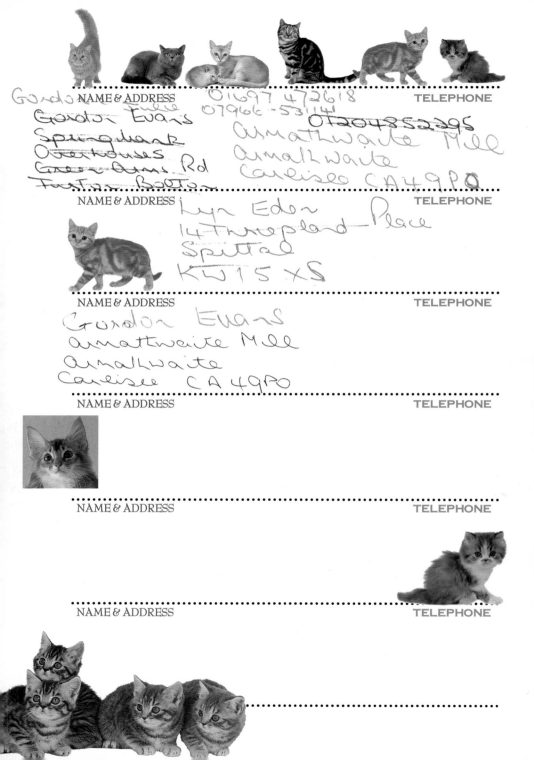

NAME & ADDRESS   **TELEPHONE**

Gordon Evans   01697 472618
Gordon Evans   07966-531141
Springbank   01204852295
Otterhouses   Armathwaite Mill
Green Arms Rd   Armathwaite
Turton Bolton   Carlisle CA4 9PO

NAME & ADDRESS   **TELEPHONE**

Lyn Eden
14 Throopland Place
Spittal
KW15 XS

NAME & ADDRESS   **TELEPHONE**

Gordon Evans
Armathwaite Mill
Armathwaite
Carlisle CA4 9PO

NAME & ADDRESS   **TELEPHONE**

NAME & ADDRESS   **TELEPHONE**

NAME & ADDRESS   **TELEPHONE**

THE HOME OF Ernest Hemingway, the American author, was overrun with 30 cats. Eventually his wife Mary, insisted on having a separate 'White Tower' built for them, which contained feeding, sleeping and even maternity facilities for them. When Hemingway died, he left behind him a whole colony of cats.

In 1963, an American doctor bequeathed $415,000 to his two cats Brownie and Hellcat.

No matter how much cats fight, there always seem to be plenty of kittens.
US President Abraham Lincoln

E

NAME & ADDRESS

TELEPHONE

NAME & ADDRESS

TELEPHONE

NAME & ADDRESS

TELEPHONE

NAME & ADDRESS

TELEPHONE

NAME & ADDRESS

TELEPHONE

NAME & ADDRESS

TELEPHONE

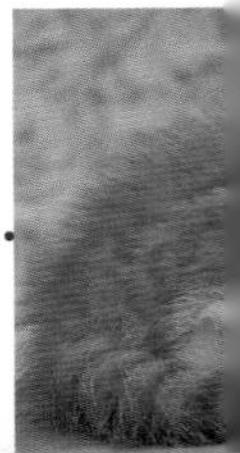

NAME & ADDRESS   TELEPHONE

NAME & ADDRESS   TELEPHONE

NAME & ADDRESS   TELEPHONE

NAME & ADDRESS   TELEPHONE

NAME & ADDRESS   TELEPHONE

NAME & ADDRESS   TELEPHONE

NAME & ADDRESS   TELEPHONE

NAME & ADDRESS   TELEPHONE

NAME & ADDRESS   TELEPHONE

NAME & ADDRESS   TELEPHONE

NAME & ADDRESS   TELEPHONE

ME & ADDRESS   TELEPHONE

IN THE 1970S, a cat called Andy, pet of US Senator Ken Myer, fell from the 16th floor of a Florida apartment building – and survived. This feat gained him the world record for the longest non-lethal fall in feline history.

The only subject on which Montmorency and I have any serious difference of opinion is cats. I like cats; Montmorency does not.

Jerome K. Jerome

E

NAME & ADDRESS   TELEPHONE

NAME & ADDRESS   TELEPHONE

NAME & ADDRESS   TELEPHONE

NAME & ADDRESS   TELEPHONE

NAME & ADDRESS   TELEPHONE

NAME & ADDRESS   TELEPHONE

THE CAT FLAP came into being in the seventeenth century – Sir Isaac Newton invented it for his cat and her kittens.

The term 'Tabby' is believed to come from the word 'Atabi' – the local word for a silken-type of material made in Baghdad. The material is characterized by its wavy markings.

F

NAME & ADDRESS   TELEPHONE

NAME & ADDRESS   TELEPHONE

NAME & ADDRESS   TELEPHONE

NAME & ADDRESS   TELEPHONE

NAME & ADDRESS   TELEPHONE

NAME & ADDRESS   TELEPHONE

NAME & ADDRESS   TELEPHONE

NAME & ADDRESS   TELEPHONE

NAME & ADDRESS   TELEPHONE

NAME & ADDRESS   TELEPHONE

NAME & ADDRESS   TELEPHONE

NAME & ADDRESS   TELEPHONE

NAME & ADDRESS   TELEPHONE

NAME & ADDRESS   TELEPHONE

NAME & ADDRESS   TELEPHONE

NAME & ADDRESS   TELEPHONE

NAME & ADDRESS   TELEPHONE

NAME & ADDRESS   TELEPHONE

HE SCORNED THE inarticulate mouthings of the lower animals. The vulgar mewing and howling of the cat species was beneath him; he sometimes uttered a sort of well-bred and articulate ejaculation, when he wished to call attention to something that he considered remarkable, or to some want of his, but he never went whining about.
Charles Dudley Warner

The poor cat had dreadful stomach-ache, and could only eat thirty-five mullet in tomato sauce, and four helpings of tripe garnished with Parmesan cheese.
Carlo Collodi

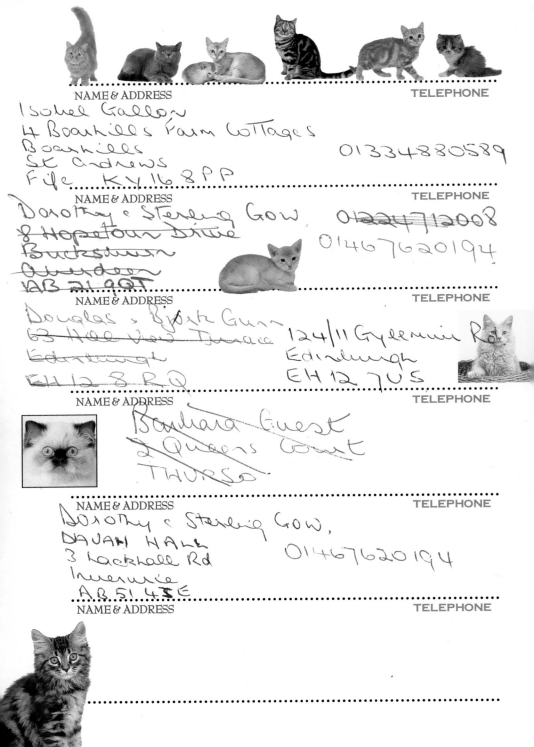

NAME & ADDRESS   **TELEPHONE**

Isobel Gallon
4 Boarhills Farm Cottages
Boarhills   01334880589
St Andrews
Fife   KY16 8PP

NAME & ADDRESS   **TELEPHONE**

Dorothy & Sterling Gow   ~~01224712008~~
8 Hopetoun Drive   01467620194
Buckstburn
~~Aberdeen~~
~~AB21 9QT~~

NAME & ADDRESS   **TELEPHONE**

Douglas & Bjørk Gunn
~~63 Hill View Terrace~~   124/11 Gylemuir Rd
~~Edinburgh~~   Edinburgh
~~EH12 8RQ~~   EH12 7US

NAME & ADDRESS   **TELEPHONE**

Barbara Guest
2 Queens Court
THURSO

NAME & ADDRESS   **TELEPHONE**

Dorothy & Sterling Gow,
DAVAH HALL   01467620194
3 Lockhall Rd
Inverurie
AB51 4JE

NAME & ADDRESS   **TELEPHONE**

MOST CATS SLEEP for about 16 hours a day – twice as much as the average human. Cats sleep erratically throughout a 24 hour period rather than in one long spell like humans. There are three types of feline sleep: the quick nap which normally lasts about half an hour; the light sleep; and the deep sleep. These last two often alternate, as the cat drifts from the first, lasting about half an hour, to the second, which lasts only six or seven minutes. It is during the short periods of deep sleep that the cat will twitch and make noises as though it were dreaming.

All cats love a cushioned couch.
Theocritus

G

NAME & ADDRESS   TELEPHONE

NAME & ADDRESS   TELEPHONE

NAME & ADDRESS   TELEPHONE

NAME & ADDRESS   TELEPHONE

NAME & ADDRESS   TELEPHONE

NAME & ADDRESS   TELEPHONE

SHE SCRATCHES her neck with a foot of rapid delight, leaning her head towards it, and shutting her eyes, half to accommodate the action of the skin, and half to enjoy the luxury.
J. H. Leigh Hunt

If you pay money for a cat it will never catch mice for you.
Traditional

NAME & ADDRESS   TELEPHONE

NAME & ADDRESS   TELEPHONE

NAME & ADDRESS   TELEPHONE

NAME & ADDRESS   TELEPHONE

NAME & ADDRESS   TELEPHONE

NAME & ADDRESS   TELEPHONE

NAME & ADDRESS

NAME & ADDRESS   TELEPHONE

NAME & ADDRESS   TELEPHONE

NAME & ADDRESS   TELEPHONE

NAME & ADDRESS   TELEPHONE

NAME & ADDRESS   TELEPHONE

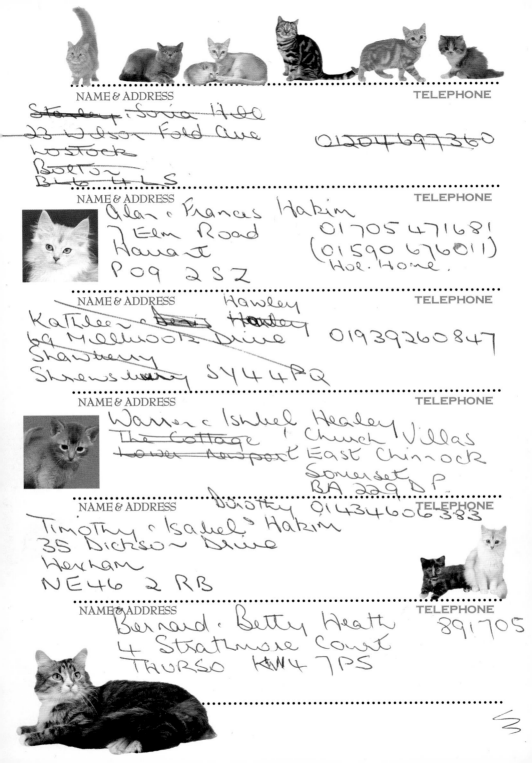

NAME & ADDRESS — **TELEPHONE**

~~Stanley~~ Jovia Hall
~~23 Udsor~~ Fold Ave
~~Lostock~~
~~Bolton~~
~~Bl6 4LS~~
01204 697360

NAME & ADDRESS — **TELEPHONE**

Alan & Frances Hakim
7 Elm Road
Havant
PO9 2SZ
01705 471681
(01590 676011)
Hol. Home.

NAME & ADDRESS — **TELEPHONE**

Kathleen ~~& Denis~~ ~~Howley~~ Howley
69 Millbrook Drive
Shawberry
Shrewsbury SY4 4PQ
01939 260847

NAME & ADDRESS — **TELEPHONE**

Warren & Isobel Healey
~~The Cottage~~ 4 Church Villas
~~Lower~~ ~~Newport~~ East Chinnock
Somerset P
BA 22 9 DP

NAME & ADDRESS — **TELEPHONE**

Dorothy 01434 606 383
Timothy & Isabel Hakim
35 Dickson Drive
Hexham
NE46 2RB

NAME & ADDRESS — **TELEPHONE**

Bernard & Betty Heath
4 Strathmore Court
THURSO KW14 7PS
891705

3

ALEXANDRE DUMAS (1823–1895), author of *The Three Musketeers*, founded the 'Feline Defence League'; one of his co-founders was fellow writer Guy de Maupassant (1850–1893).

British Prime Minister Winston Churchill adopted a stray black cat that turned up on the doorstep of No. 10 Downing Street, thinking it was a sign of good luck. He christened it Margate, having just returned from delivering an important speech in that town.

NAME & ADDRESS   TELEPHONE

NAME & ADDRESS   TELEPHONE

NAME & ADDRESS   TELEPHONE

NAME & ADDRESS   TELEPHONE

NAME & ADDRESS   TELEPHONE

NAME & ADDRESS   TELEPHONE

THEY EAT SLOWLY, *and are peculiarly fond of fish. They drink frequently; their sleep is light; and they often assume the appearance of sleeping, when in reality they are meditating mischief. They walk softly, and without making any noise. As their hair is always dry, it easily gives out an electrical fire, which becomes visible when rubbed across in the dark. Their eyes likewise sparkle in the dark like diamonds. The cat, when pleased, purrs, and moves its tail: when angry, it spits, hisses, and strikes with its foot.*

Encyclopedia Britannica, 1787

NAME & ADDRESS   TELEPHONE

NAME & ADDRESS   TELEPHONE

NAME & ADDRESS   TELEPHONE

NAME & ADDRESS   TELEPHONE

NAME & ADDRESS   TELEPHONE

NAME & ADDRESS   TELEPHONE

NAME & ADDRESS   TELEPHONE

NAME & ADDRESS   TELEPHONE

....

NAME & ADDRESS   TELEPHONE

H

NAME & ADDRESS   TELEPHONE

NAME & ADDRESS   TELEPHONE

NAME & ADDRESS   TELEPHONE

NAME & ADDRESS   TELEPHONE

NAME & ADDRESS   TELEPHONE

NAME & ADDRESS   TELEPHONE

NAME & ADDRESS   TELEPHONE

NAME & ADDRESS   TELEPHONE

NAME & ADDRESS   TELEPHONE

NAME & ADDRESS   TELEPHONE

FOR I WILL consider my cat Jeoffrey
. . . . For he is of the tribe of tiger . .
. . For he will not do destruction, if
he is well-fed, neither will
he spit without
provocation . . . . For he is
an instrument for the
children to learn
benevolence upon . . . . For
every house is incompleat
without him
. . . . For he is the cleanest
in the use of his fore-paws
of any quadrupede . . . .
For he is the quickest to
the mark of any creature.
For he is tenacious of his
point. For he is a mixture
of gravery and waggery
. . . . For there is nothing
sweeter than his peace when
at rest. For there is nothing
brisker than his life when in
motion.

Christopher Smart

NAME & ADDRESS   TELEPHONE

NAME & ADDRESS   TELEPHONE

NAME & ADDRESS   TELEPHONE

NAME & ADDRESS   TELEPHONE

NAME & ADDRESS   TELEPHONE

NAME & ADDRESS   TELEPHONE

NAME & ADDRESS   TELEPHONE

....

NAME & ADDRESS   TELEPHONE

NAME & ADDRESS   TELEPHONE

NAME & ADDRESS   TELEPHONE

NAME & ADDRESS   TELEPHONE

....

NAME & ADDRESS   TELEPHONE

....

NAME & ADDRESS

TELEPHONE

NAME & ADDRESS

TELEPHONE

NAME & ADDRESS

TELEPHONE

NAME & ADDRESS

TELEPHONE

NAME & ADDRESS

TELEPHONE

NAME & ADDRESS

TELEPHONE

THE THIRD EARL of Southampton had a cat named Trixie. It is believed that when the Earl was imprisoned during the reign of Queen Elizabeth I, his cat found its way to his cell and climbed down the chimney. There it remained as his companion until he was released.

Cats are not impure; they keep watch about us.
The Prophet Mohammad

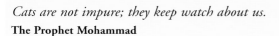

H Kerr
17 Braeside Park
Balloch
INVERNESS
IV2 7HL

NAME & ADDRESS   (MrsH Kerr)   **TELEPHONE**

Tricia & ~~Jimmy~~ Kerr
17 Braeside Park
Balloch
Inverness IV2 7HL

01463794088

NAME & ADDRESS   **TELEPHONE**

NAME & ADDRESS   **TELEPHONE**

NAME & ADDRESS   **TELEPHONE**

NAME & ADDRESS   **TELEPHONE**

NAME & ADDRESS   **TELEPHONE**

THE LONGEST SERVING mouser at No. 10 Downing Street was a large black and white cat named Wilberforce. Wilberforce saw many Prime Ministers of Britain come and go, including Edward Heath, Harold Wilson, James Callaghan and Margaret Thatcher.

Hywel Dda, the Prince of Wales in AD 936, felt that domestic cats played such an important role as controller of vermin that they deserved more respect, and he thus introduced special laws to protect them, including fixed penalties for stealing or killing a cat.

K

NAME & ADDRESS   TELEPHONE

NAME & ADDRESS   TELEPHONE

NAME & ADDRESS   TELEPHONE

NAME & ADDRESS   TELEPHONE

NAME & ADDRESS   TELEPHONE

NAME & ADDRESS   TELEPHONE

I SHALL NEVER FORGET the indulgence with which he [Dr Johnson] treated Hodge, his cat: for whom he himself used to go out and buy oysters, lest the servants having that trouble should take a dislike to the poor creature.

James Boswell, ***The Life of Samuel Johnson***

If a cat dies in a private house by a natural death, all the inmates of the house shave their eyebrows.

Herodotus

K

NAME & ADDRESS   TELEPHONE

. . . .
NAME & ADDRESS   TELEPHONE

. . . .
NAME & ADDRESS   TELEPHONE

. . . .
NAME & ADDRESS   TELEPHONE

. . . .
NAME & ADDRESS   TELEPHONE

. . . .
NAME & ADDRESS   TELEPHONE

. . . .

NAME & ADDRESS TELEPHONE

NAME & ADDRESS TELEPHONE

NAME & ADDRESS TELEPHONE

K

NAME & ADDRESS TELEPHONE

NAME & ADDRESS TELEPHONE

NAME & ADDRESS TELEPHONE

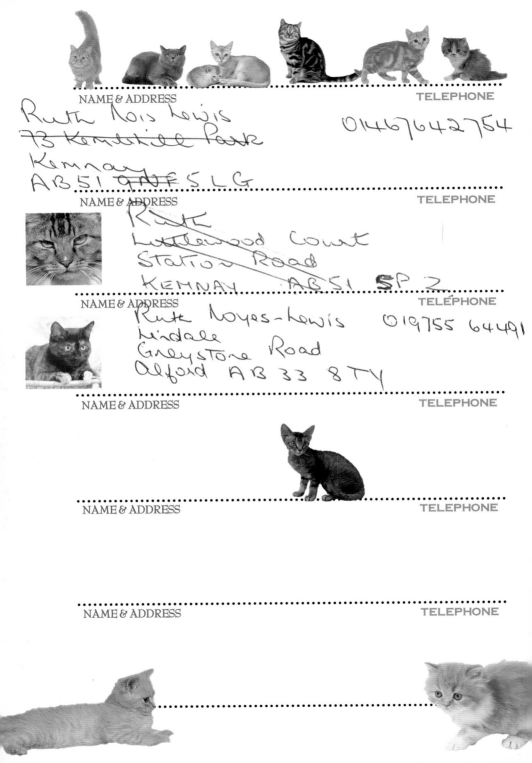

NAME & ADDRESS **TELEPHONE**

Ruth Lois Lewis
73 Kembhill Park
Kemnay
AB51 ~~GNF~~ 5LG

01467642754

NAME & ADDRESS **TELEPHONE**

Ruth
Littlewood Court
Station Road
KEMNAY   AB51 5PZ

NAME & ADDRESS **TELEPHONE**

Ruth Noyes-Lewis
Lindale
Greystone Road
Alford AB33 8TY

019755 64491

NAME & ADDRESS **TELEPHONE**

NAME & ADDRESS **TELEPHONE**

NAME & ADDRESS **TELEPHONE**

BRITISH PRIME MINISTER Winston Churchill was a renowned cat lover. A special chair was kept for his favourite cat, both in the Cabinet Room and at Churchill's dining table. For many years his favourite cat was the aptly named Nelson who, as well as sitting beside his master, also shared his bed. In later years, the favoured cat was one named Jock. Jock outlived Churchill and was among the named beneficiaries of his will.

When I made the acquaintance of Tobermory a week ago I saw at once that I was in contact with a 'Beyond-Cat' of extraordinary intelligence.
Saki

L

NAME & ADDRESS   TELEPHONE

NAME & ADDRESS   TELEPHONE

NAME & ADDRESS   TELEPHONE

NAME & ADDRESS   TELEPHONE

NAME & ADDRESS   TELEPHONE

NAME & ADDRESS   TELEPHONE

NAME & ADDRESS   TELEPHONE

NAME & ADDRESS   TELEPHONE

NAME & ADDRESS   TELEPHONE

NAME & ADDRESS   TELEPHONE

L

NAME & ADDRESS   TELEPHONE

NAME & ADDRESS   TELEPHONE

NAME & ADDRESS   TELEPHONE

NAME & ADDRESS   TELEPHONE

NAME & ADDRESS   TELEPHONE

NAME & ADDRESS   TELEPHONE

NAME & ADDRESS   TELEPHONE

NAME & ADDRESS   TELEPHONE

IN FEBRUARY 1909, the Keeper of Egyptian cat mummies at the British Museum in London found a tiny kitten. It was taken in and looked after by the museum staff, who named him Mike. Mike happily hunted pigeons at the British Museum for 20 years.

The cat would eat fish but would not wet her feet.
Proverb

L

NAME & ADDRESS — **TELEPHONE**

Chrissie Mackay
Culdin
KinTessack
Forres
IV 36 OTL

NAME & ADDRESS — **TELEPHONE**

Pauline Morton   01709 542440
38 The Brow
Brecks
Rotherham   S65 3HP
S. Yorks

NAME & ADDRESS — **TELEPHONE**

Dan e Docina Mackenzie
Au-Ren HOUSE
Bannock

NAME & ADDRESS — **TELEPHONE**

Jacqueline McMillan   01369 701712
Flat 2   07871831342
No 9 Argyll Terrace
Kirn
Dunoon   PA23 8LR

NAME & ADDRESS — **TELEPHONE**

NAME & ADDRESS — **TELEPHONE**

THE COMPOSER Frédéric Chopin (1810–1849) claimed his *Valse brilliante* in A minor, opus 34. no. 3 (also known as his 'Cat Waltz') was partially inspired by his pet cat, which jumped on to his keyboard while he was composing it.

Sir Andrew Lloyd Webber's stage musical *Cats* (inspired by the poetry of T. S. Eliot) has been performed in 13 countries and in 10 languages.

M

NAME & ADDRESS   TELEPHONE

NAME & ADDRESS   TELEPHONE

NAME & ADDRESS   TELEPHONE

NAME & ADDRESS   TELEPHONE

NAME & ADDRESS   TELEPHONE

NAME & ADDRESS   TELEPHONE

A CAT CAME fiddling out of a barn,
With a pair of bag-pipes under her arm;
She could sing nothing but, Fiddle cum fee,
The mouse has married the humble-bee.
Pipe, cat; dance, mouse;
We'll have a wedding at our good house.
Wiltshire Manuscript, 1740

They were at play, she and her cat,
And it was marvellous to mark
The white paw and the white hand pat
Each other in the deepening dark.
Paul Verlaine

NAME & ADDRESS

TELEPHONE

NAME & ADDRESS

TELEPHONE

NAME & ADDRESS

TELEPHONE

NAME & ADDRESS

TELEPHONE

NAME & ADDRESS

TELEPHONE

NAME & ADDRESS

TELEPHONE

NAME & ADDRESS   TELEPHONE

NAME & ADDRESS   TELEPHONE

NAME & ADDRESS   TELEPHONE

NAME & ADDRESS   TELEPHONE

M

NAME & ADDRESS   TELEPHONE

NAME & ADDRESS   TELEPHONE

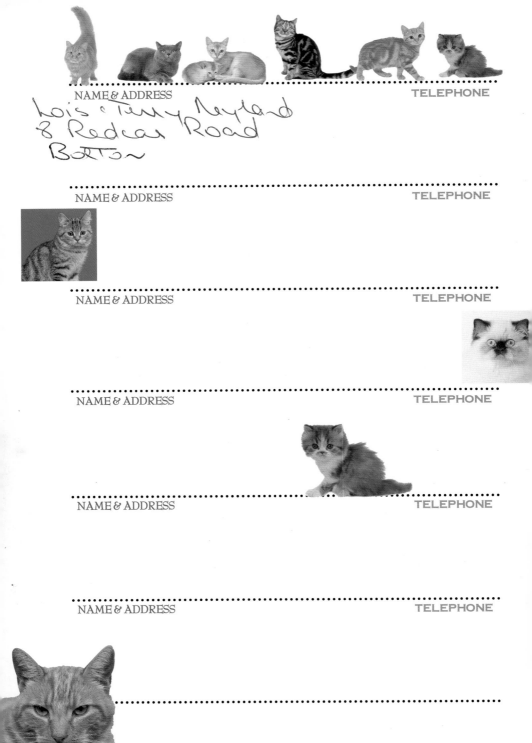

NAME & ADDRESS

TELEPHONE

Lois & Terry Nayland
8 Redcar Road
Bolton

NAME & ADDRESS

TELEPHONE

NAME & ADDRESS

TELEPHONE

NAME & ADDRESS

TELEPHONE

NAME & ADDRESS

TELEPHONE

NAME & ADDRESS

TELEPHONE

THE 18TH-CENTURY diary of the **Rev. James Woodforde** records the following cure for a sty on the eyelid: *'It is commonly said that the eyelid being rubbed by the tail of a black Cat, would do much good, if not entirely cure it.'* The Reverend tried this himself and wrote that *'very soon after dinner I found my Eyelid much abated of the swelling and almost free from pain.'*

In Japan an effigy of a Beckoning Cat, *maneki-neko*, is thought to bring good luck and to provide protection.

NAME & ADDRESS　　　　　　　　　　　　　　　　TELEPHONE

NAME & ADDRESS　　　　　　　　　　　　　　　　TELEPHONE

NAME & ADDRESS　　　　　　　　　　　　　　　　TELEPHONE

NAME & ADDRESS　　　　　　　　　　　　　　　　TELEPHONE

NAME & ADDRESS　　　　　　　　　　　　　　　　TELEPHONE

NAME & ADDRESS　　　　　　　　　　　　　　　　TELEPHONE

NAME & ADDRESS

NAME & ADDRESS

TELEPHONE

NAME & ADDRESS

TELEPHONE

NAME & ADDRESS

TELEPHONE

NAME & ADDRESS

TELEPHONE

NAME & ADDRESS

TELEPHONE

NAME & ADDRESS   TELEPHONE

NAME & ADDRESS   TELEPHONE

NAME & ADDRESS   TELEPHONE

NAME & ADDRESS   TELEPHONE

NAME & ADDRESS   TELEPHONE

NAME & ADDRESS   TELEPHONE

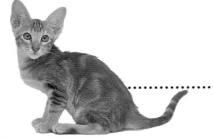

WHEN SHE WALKED . . . she stretched out long and thin like a little tiger, and held her head high to look over the grass as if she were threading the jungle.
Sarah Orne Jewett

What sort of philosophers are we, that know absolutely nothing of the origins and destiny of cats?
Henry David Thoreau

NAME & ADDRESS **TELEPHONE**

Ken Pickering
27 Chelgrove Ave
Blackrod
Bolton BL6 5TR

01204 696137

NAME & ADDRESS **TELEPHONE**

Julie Patterson (& Andy)
Filloway Cottage
Berriock
THURSO

NAME & ADDRESS **TELEPHONE**

Christine & Evan Park
20 ~~Hot~~ Howburn Rd
Thurso

NAME & ADDRESS **TELEPHONE**

NAME & ADDRESS **TELEPHONE**

NAME & ADDRESS **TELEPHONE**

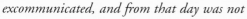

IN SCANDINAVIA there are stories of a mythical cat, known as the Butter Cat. The Butter Cat is protective and a provider of gifts, especially milk and butter.

The Vicar of Morwenstow was usually followed to church by nine or ten cats, which entered the chancel with him, and careered about it during service. Originally ten cats accompanied him to church; but one, having caught, killed, and eaten a mouse on a Sunday, was excommunicated, and from that day was not allowed again within the sanctuary.

Sabine Baring-Gould (1834–1924), *The Vicar of Morwenstow*

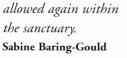

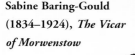

NAME & ADDRESS   TELEPHONE

NAME & ADDRESS   TELEPHONE

NAME & ADDRESS   TELEPHONE

NAME & ADDRESS   TELEPHONE

NAME & ADDRESS   TELEPHONE

NAME & ADDRESS   TELEPHONE

IF A CAT sneezes near a bride on her wedding morning, her happiness is assured.
Traditional

Finally she gave a sneeze, and another twist of mouth and whiskers, and then, curling her tail towards her front claws settled herself on her hind quarters in an attitude of bland meditation.
J. H. Leigh Hunt

OF

NAME & ADDRESS   TELEPHONE

....

NAME & ADDRESS   TELEPHONE

NAME & ADDRESS   TELEPHONE

NAME & ADDRESS   TELEPHONE

NAME & ADDRESS   TELEPHONE

NAME & ADDRESS   TELEPHONE

NAME & ADDRESS　　　　　　　　　　　　　　　　　　TELEPHONE

NAME & ADDRESS　　　　　　　　　　　　　　　　　　TELEPHONE

NAME & ADDRESS　　　　　　　　　　　　　　　　　　TELEPHONE

NAME & ADDRESS　　　　　　　　　　　　　　　　　　TELEPHONE

OP

NAME & ADDRESS　　　　　　　　　　　　　　　　　　TELEPHONE

NAME & ADDRESS　　　　　　　　　　　　　　　　　　TELEPHONE

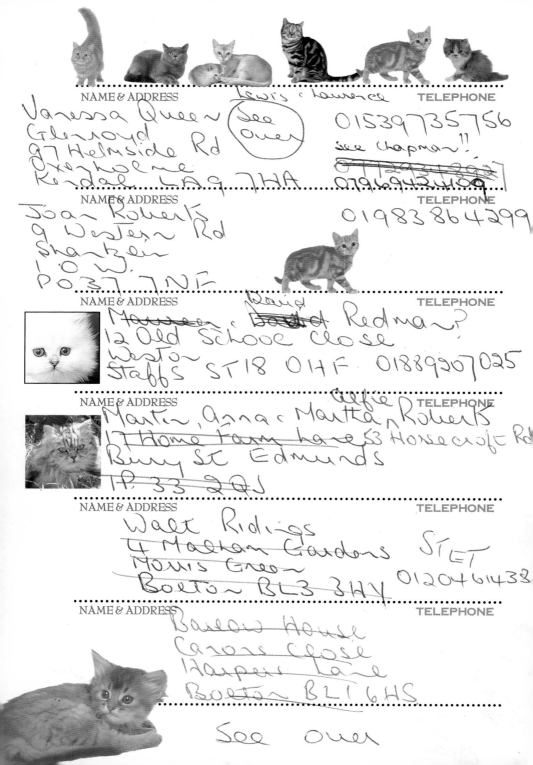

NAME & ADDRESS — Lewis Laurence **TELEPHONE**

Vanessa Queen
Glenroyd   (See Over)   01539735756
97 Helmside Rd   see chapman !!
Oxenholme
Kendal LA9 7HA   ~~01539 728~~ 07969432400

NAME & ADDRESS **TELEPHONE**

Joan Roberts   01983 864299
9 Western Rd
Shanklin
I.O.W.
PO37 7NF

NAME & ADDRESS — David **TELEPHONE**

~~Maureen~~ ~~David~~ Redman ?
12 Old School Close
Weston
Staffs ST18 0HF   01889907025

NAME & ADDRESS — Alfie **TELEPHONE**

Martin, Anna & Martha Roberts
~~17 Home Farm Lane~~ 53 Horsecroft Rd
Bury St Edmunds
IP33 2QJ

NAME & ADDRESS **TELEPHONE**

Walt Ridings
4 Maldon Gardens   STET
~~Morris Green~~   0120461438
Bolton BL3 3HY

NAME & ADDRESS **TELEPHONE**

Bailow House
Carons Close
Harpers Lane
Bolton BL1 6HS

See over

FLORENCE NIGHTINGALE owned 60 cats throughout her lifetime, and always travelled with her favourites.

The nature of this beast is to love the place of her breeding; neither will she tarry in any strange place, although carried far. She is never willing to forsake the love of any man, and this is contrary to the nature of a dog, who will travel abroad with his master. Although their masters forsake their houses, yet will not cats bear them company, and being carried forth in close baskets or sacks, they will return again or lose themselves.

John Topsell

QR

NAME & ADDRESS

Vanessa Queen
Bank Head Farm
Underbarrow Road
Kendal Cumbria
LA8 8HA

TELEPHONE

01539 721785

(John)

Lewis's house ~
Robilele

NAME & ADDRESS

TELEPHONE

NAME & ADDRESS

TELEPHONE

NAME & ADDRESS

TELEPHONE

NAME & ADDRESS

TELEPHONE

NAME & ADDRESS

TELEPHONE

NAME & ADDRESS   TELEPHONE

. . . .

NAME & ADDRESS   TELEPHONE

. . . .

NAME & ADDRESS   TELEPHONE

NAME & ADDRESS   TELEPHONE

. . . .

NAME & ADDRESS   TELEPHONE

. . . .

NAME & ADDRESS   TELEPHONE

. . . .

NAME & ADDRESS   TELEPHONE

NAME & ADDRESS   TELEPHONE

NAME & ADDRESS   TELEPHONE

NAME & ADDRESS   TELEPHONE

NAME & ADDRESS   TELEPHONE

NAME & ADDRESS   TELEPHONE

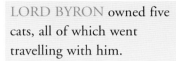

LORD BYRON owned five cats, all of which went travelling with him.

Long contact with the human race has developed in [the cat] the art of diplomacy, and no Roman Cardinal of medieval days knew better how to ingratiate himself with his surroundings than a cat with a saucer of cream on its mental horizon.

Saki, *The Achievement of the Cat*

NAME & ADDRESS **TELEPHONE**

~~Liz Surham
18 Deon St
Stockbridge
Edinburgh~~

NAME & ADDRESS **TELEPHONE**

Joan ~~& Peter~~ Smith
Gowan Croft
Staveley
Kendal   LA8 9NE   01539 821058
Cumbria

NAME & ADDRESS **TELEPHONE**

Marlene Sutherland
12 Ormlie Drive
THURSO   890227
KW14 7BA   07843 22900

NAME & ADDRESS **TELEPHONE**

NAME & ADDRESS **TELEPHONE**

NAME & ADDRESS **TELEPHONE**

DETECTIVE WRITER Raymond Chandler called his black Persian, Taki, his 'feline secretary'. She was always the first to hear his novels as Chandler read his drafts aloud to her.

The English poet and author Robert Southey gave his cat the title: The Most Noble the Archduke Rumpelstizchen, Marquis Macbum, Earl Tomemange, Baron Raticide, Waowler, and Skaratchi.

Charles Dickens owned a white cat that he called William. When William produced a litter of kittens, however, he was quickly renamed Williamina.

S

NAME & ADDRESS   TELEPHONE

NAME & ADDRESS   TELEPHONE

NAME & ADDRESS   TELEPHONE

NAME & ADDRESS   TELEPHONE

NAME & ADDRESS   TELEPHONE

NAME & ADDRESS   TELEPHONE

I AND PANGUR BÁN my cat
'Tis a like task we are at
Hunting mice is his delight
Hunting words I sit all night.

So in peace our tasks we play,
Pangur Bán, my cat, and I;
In our arts we find our bliss,
I have mine and he has his.

Irish Scholar, 8th Century

S

NAME & ADDRESS   TELEPHONE

....

NAME & ADDRESS   TELEPHONE

....

NAME & ADDRESS   TELEPHONE

....

NAME & ADDRESS   TELEPHONE

....

NAME & ADDRESS   TELEPHONE

....

NAME & ADDRESS   TELEPHONE

....

NAME & ADDRESS   TELEPHONE

NAME & ADDRESS   TELEPHONE

NAME & ADDRESS   TELEPHONE

NAME & ADDRESS   TELEPHONE

NAME & ADDRESS   TELEPHONE

S

NAME & ADDRESS   TELEPHONE

NAME & ADDRESS   **TELEPHONE**

Lena Taylor
11 Forge Head Ave
Hall i'th Wood
Bolton BL1 8F2

NAME & ADDRESS   **TELEPHONE**

Col Trueman
17 Aintree Lane
Liverpool
102 5 3.

NAME & ADDRESS   **TELEPHONE**

Kathleen Thornton
10 Kingsway Close
Kingsway
Ossett WF5 8DY
W. Yorks

NAME & ADDRESS   **TELEPHONE**

NAME & ADDRESS   **TELEPHONE**

NAME & ADDRESS   **TELEPHONE**

DURING MARGARET THATCHER'S time as Prime Minister of Britain, an adopted stray called Humphrey became the official mouser of No. 10 Downing Street. He remained there throughout John Major's premiership, apart from a short period in which he disappeared and was believed to have died. It later transpired that he had been taken in by the local Royal Army Medical College, situated not far from Downing Street, who returned Humphrey as soon as his identity became known.

T

NAME & ADDRESS   TELEPHONE

NAME & ADDRESS   TELEPHONE

NAME & ADDRESS   TELEPHONE

NAME & ADDRESS   TELEPHONE

NAME & ADDRESS   TELEPHONE

NAME & ADDRESS   TELEPHONE

NAME & ADDRESS   TELEPHONE

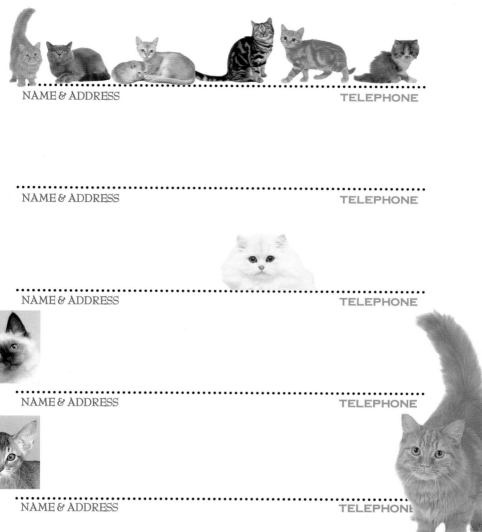

NAME & ADDRESS   TELEPHONE

NAME & ADDRESS   TELEPHONE

NAME & ADDRESS   TELEPHONE

NAME & ADDRESS   TELEPHONE

NAME & ADDRESS   TELEPHONE

T

NAME & ADDRESS   TELEPHONE

NAME & ADDRESS   TELEPHONE

NAME & ADDRESS   TELEPHONE

NAME & ADDRESS   TELEPHONE

NAME & ADDRESS   TELEPHONE

NAME & ADDRESS   TELEPHONE

NAME & ADDRESS   TELEPHONE

ALdoJTHOUGH CATS LIVE *in our houses, they can hardly be called domestic animals; they may rather be said to enjoy full liberty; for they never act but according to their own inclination.*
Encyclopedia Britannica

Like the rest of nobility, she is much given to hunting, birding and fishing but hates all other sorts of exertion.
Thomas Brown

T

NAME & ADDRESS   TELEPHONE

NAME & ADDRESS   TELEPHONE

NAME & ADDRESS   TELEPHONE

NAME & ADDRESS   TELEPHONE

NAME & ADDRESS   TELEPHONE

NAME & ADDRESS   TELEPHONE

AT BIRTH, kittens are both blind and deaf, but they have a strong sense of smell and touch which enables them to find their mother's nipples to feed. At three weeks, the kittens' eyes are fully open and they are beginning to crawl about. At one month they will begin to show signs of playing with one another and their teeth will have started to come through. At this stage they will also have their first taste of solid food, although they will not be weaned from their mother for a further month.

I have a kitten . . . the drollest of all creatures that ever wore a cat's skin.
William Cowper

UV

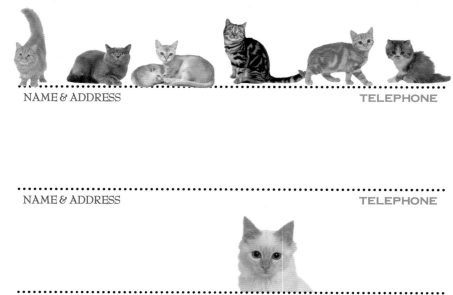

NAME & ADDRESS   TELEPHONE

....

NAME & ADDRESS   TELEPHONE

....

NAME & ADDRESS   TELEPHONE

....

NAME & ADDRESS   TELEPHONE

....

NAME & ADDRESS   TELEPHONE

....

NAME & ADDRESS   TELEPHONE

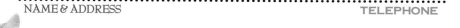

THE PLAYFUL KITTEN, with its pretty tigerish gambols, is infinitely more amusing than half the people one is obliged to live with in the world.
Lady Sidney Morgan

Wild beasts he created later,
Lions with their paws so furious;
In the image of the lion
Made he kittens small and curious.
Heinrich Heine

UV

NAME & ADDRESS   TELEPHONE

....

NAME & ADDRESS   TELEPHONE

....

NAME & ADDRESS   TELEPHONE

....

NAME & ADDRESS   TELEPHONE

....

NAME & ADDRESS   TELEPHONE

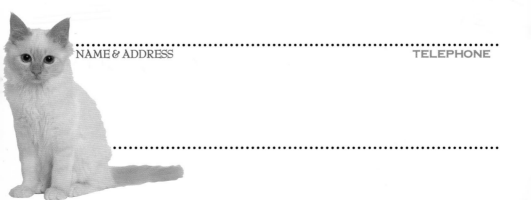

....

NAME & ADDRESS   TELEPHONE

....

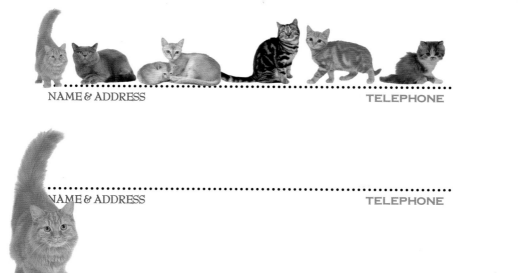

NAME & ADDRESS   TELEPHONE

....
NAME & ADDRESS   TELEPHONE

....
NAME & ADDRESS   TELEPHONE

....
NAME & ADDRESS   TELEPHONE

....
NAME & ADDRESS   TELEPHONE

....
NAME & ADDRESS   TELEP

UV

....

NAME & ADDRESS — **TELEPHONE**

Ros. Bruce, Jamie & Stephen Worsley
Foxhole Bank
Crosthwaite
Kendal Cumbria
LA8 8AN
0153956836

NAME & ADDRESS — **TELEPHONE**

Elsie & Jack Wood
26 Meadowside Close
Low Park
Endmoor
Kendal Cumbria
01539560048

NAME & ADDRESS — **TELEPHONE**

Meeling Whitehead
Kirkside Cottage
Stenton
East Lothian
EH42 1TE
01368850628

NAME & ADDRESS — **TELEPHONE**

Anne Row Wilmott
18 Brightwell Drive
Leicester Forest East
Leicester
LE3 3QA
01646600053

NAME & ADDRESS — **TELEPHONE**

Joan & Tony Whitaker
Mandor 12 Paley Close
Castletown Marton
Blackpool FY4 4XS
Lancs
821322
01253 318140

NAME & ADDRESS — **TELEPHONE**

Mr & Mrs P. Welsh
The White House
Ford Road
Wiveliscombe
Taunton
Somerset TA4 2RQ
01984 623394

EMILY BRONTË owned a cat called Tiger, which played at her feet throughout the writing of *Wuthering Heights*.

In the film *Breakfast at Tiffany's* (1961), Audrey Hepburn's feline co-star, simply called 'Cat' in the film, was actually a professional ginger tom called 'Orangey'.

Thomas Hardy, the nineteenth-century novelist, was a great cat-lover, so much so that when his much-loved pet died, he buried it under its favourite tree. He then wrote a long poem dedicated to his mourned cat.

NAME & ADDRESS   TELEPHONE

··

NAME & ADDRESS   TELEPHONE

··

NAME & ADDRESS   TELEPHONE

··

NAME & ADDRESS   TELEPHONE

··

NAME & ADDRESS   TELEPHONE

··

NAME & ADDRESS   TELEPHONE

··

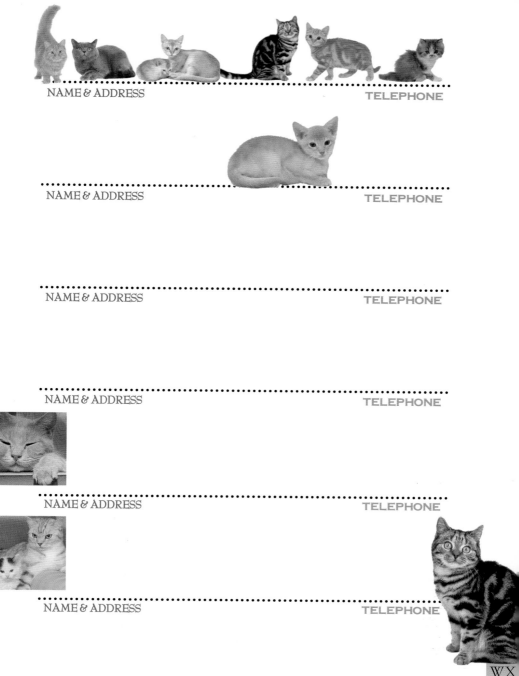

NAME & ADDRESS · TELEPHONE

NAME & ADDRESS · TELEPHONE

NAME & ADDRESS · TELEPHONE

NAME & ADDRESS · TELEPHONE

NAME & ADDRESS · TELEPHONE

NAME & ADDRESS · TELEPHONE

WX

NAME & ADDRESS

TELEPHONE

NAME & ADDRESS

TELEPHONE

NAME & ADDRESS

TELEPHONE

NAME & ADDRESS

TELEPHONE

NAME & ADDRESS

TELEPHONE

NAME & ADDRESS

TELEPHONE

WE HAVE A BLACK CAT *and an old dog at the Rectory. I know somebody to whose knee that black cat loves to climb; against whose shoulder and cheek it likes to purr . . . . And what does that somebody do? He quietly strokes the cat, and lets her sit.*
Charlotte Brontë

Stately, kindly, lordly friend,
Condescend
Here to sit by me, and turn
Glorious eyes that smile and burn,
Golden eyes, love's lustrous meed,
     On the golden page I read.
       Algernon Swinburne

WX

NAME & ADDRESS — **TELEPHONE**

Stuart & ~~Frances~~ Paul
Quiet Waters
79 Kemphill Park
Kennay
AB50 9HG

01467 643804

NAME & ADDRESS — **TELEPHONE**

Jackie
~~26 Chargeltta Circle~~
~~Fraserburgh~~
~~AB43 5WH~~

7 URY HOUS
KELLANES F
INVERURIE
AB51 3RU

NAME & ADDRESS — **TELEPHONE**

Dorothy ~~Gow~~
2 North Bettelvie Cottage
~~Old Meldrum~~
~~AB51 0AN~~

NAME & ADDRESS — **TELEPHONE**

Caren & Sam Gary Yates
~~Gary~~
~~4 Fitch Place~~ ~~the~~ Morsweg 140
2332 ER ~~Heiden~~
See over. Holland.

NAME & ADDRESS — **TELEPHONE**

Roy & Kay Meadow
Hazy Meadow
Meadow Park Drive
Burrington
Umberleigh EX37 9TY

NAME & ADDRESS — **TELEPHONE**

Roy & Kay
7 Court Farm Close
Winsham
Somerset
TA20 4JY

01460 3001

THE HOLLYWOOD actress Kim Basinger demanded custody of her cats when filing for divorce.

Unconventional French novelist George Sand (1804–76) ate her breakfast from the same bowl as her cat.

Sixties' icon and Hollywood star Brigitte Bardot shares her home with some 60 stray cats. The animal-loving, retired actress also allows her cats to sleep on her bed.

NAME & ADDRESS / **TELEPHONE**

GARY ∘ CAREN YATES 'SAM'
NORSWEG 140
2332 ER LEIDEN.
HOLLAND

NAME & ADDRESS / **TELEPHONE**

Michael Yates
14106 Briarhills Pkwy
Houston, TX 77077

NAME & ADDRESS / **TELEPHONE**

NAME & ADDRESS / **TELEPHONE**

NAME & ADDRESS / **TELEPHONE**

NAME & ADDRESS / **TELEPHONE**

NAME & ADDRESS   TELEPHONE

NAME & ADDRESS   TELEPHONE

NAME & ADDRESS   TELEPHONE

NAME & ADDRESS   TELEPHONE

NAME & ADDRESS   TELEPHONE

NAME & ADDRESS   TELEPHONE

YZ

NAME & ADDRESS   TELEPHONE

NAME & ADDRESS   TELEPHONE

NAME & ADDRESS   TELEPHONE

NAME & ADDRESS   TELEPHONE

NAME & ADDRESS   TELEPHONE

NAME & ADDRESS   TELEPHONE

SHE WAS FOND *of luxury, and it was always upon the handsomest easy chair, or the rug that would best show off her snowy fur, that she would surely be found.*

Théophile Gautier, *The White and Black Dynasties*

I learned the lesson of life from a little kitten of mine . . . the little one stands her ground; and when the old enemy comes near enough kisses his nose and makes the peace. That is the lesson of life; to kiss one's enemy's nose always standing one's ground.

Florence Nightingale